PIANO/CONDUCTOR, OBOE

Holiday Songs From Around
CHRISTMAS DUETS FOR ALL

Playable on ANY TWO INSTRUMENTS
or any number of instruments in ensemble

WILLIAM RYDEN

MW00805705

TABLE OF CONTENTS

THE SLEEP OF THE CHILD JESUS..........................Francois Gevaert, France..........................3
THE ANGELS AND THE SHEPHERDS..................Bohemia 4
UNTO US IS BORN A SON ....Tune from Piae Cantiones, 1592, England........4
A CHILD THIS DAY IS BORN ....England 5
O COME, O COME, EMMANUEL......................Plainsong Chant 6
IT CAME UPON THE MIDNIGHT CLEAR ....Richard S. Willis, America............................6
SILENT NIGHT ....Franz Gruber, Germany 7
O CHRISTMAS TREE (O Tannenbaum) ....Germany 8
O SANCTISSIMA ....Sicily 8
I SAW THREE SHIPS ....England 9
O COME, ALL YE FAITHFUL...........................From J.F. Wade's Cantus Diversi 10
TELL US WISE MEN.....................................Poland 10
O LITTLE TOWN OF BETHLEHEM......................Lewis H. Redner, America............................11
THE BABE IN BETHLEM'S MANGER LAID ....England 12
DECK THE HALLS ....Old Welsh 12
THE NEW BORN BABE ....Spiritual 14
GOOD KING WENCESLAS ....John Mason Neale, England.........................15
WHAT YOU GONNA CALL YOUR PRETTY
    LITTLE BABY? ....Spiritual 16
FUM, FUM, FUM! ....Catalonia 17
HARK! WHAT MEAN THOSE HOLY VOICES?.......Russian Melody 17
MASTERS IN THIS HALL ....William Morris, England............................18
BORN TODAY IS THE CHILD DIVINE (Il Est Ne) .....France 20
ROCKING...Czechoslovakia 21
MARCH OF THE THREE KINGS ....Georges Bizet, France............................22
A LA MEDIA NOCHE ....Puerto Rico 23
PATAPAN ....France 24

INSTRUMENTATION

EL9554 - Piano/Conductor, Oboe
EL9555 - Flute, Piccolo
EL9556 - B♭ Clarinet, Bass Clarinet
EL9557 - Alto Saxophone (E♭ Saxes and
      E♭ Clarinets)
EL9558 - Tenor Saxophone
EL9559 - B♭ Trumpet, Baritone T.C.

EL9560 - Horn in F
EL9561 - Trombone, Baritone B.C., Bassoon, Tuba
EL9562 - Violin
EL9563 - Viola
EL9564 - Cello/Bass
EL9565 - Percussion

Editor: Thom Proctor
Cover: Dallas Soto

L9554

ALPHABETICAL CONTENTS

A LA MEDIA NOCHE ....Puerto Rico..............................23
THE ANGELS AND THE SHEPHERDS..................Bohemia 4
THE BABE IN BETHLEM'S MANGER LAID ....England 12
BORN TODAY IS THE CHILD DIVINE (Il Est Ne) .....France..............................20
A CHILD THIS DAY IS BORN ....England..............................5
DECK THE HALLS ....Old Welsh 12
FUM, FUM, FUM! ....Catalonia..............................17
GOOD KING WENCESLAS ....John Mason Neale, England..............................15
HARK! WHAT MEAN THOSE HOLY VOICES?.......Russian Melody 17
I SAW THREE SHIPS ....England..............................9
IT CAME UPON THE MIDNIGHT CLEAR ....Richard S. Willis, America..............................6
MARCH OF THE THREE KINGS ....Georges Bizet, France..............................22
MASTERS IN THIS HALL..........................William Morris, England..............................18
THE NEW BORN BABE ....Spiritual..............................14
O CHRISTMAS TREE (O Tannenbaum) ....Germany 8
O COME, ALL YE FAITHFUL..........................From J.F. Wade's Cantus Diversi..............................10
O COME, O COME, EMMANUEL....................Plainsong Chant 6
O LITTLE TOWN OF BETHLEHEM....................Lewis H. Redner, America..............................11
O SANCTISSIMA ....Sicily 8
PATAPAN ....France..............................24
ROCKING..............................Czechoslovakia 21
SILENT NIGHT ....Franz Gruber, Germany 7
THE SLEEP OF THE CHILD JESUS....................Francois Gevaert, France..............................3
TELL US WISE MEN..............................Poland..............................10
UNTO US IS BORN A SON ....Tune from Piae Cantiones, 1592, England........4
WHAT YOU GONNA CALL YOUR PRETTY
  LITTLE BABY?..............................Spiritual..............................16

WILLIAM RYDEN was born in New York City and is a life-long resident of Forest Hills, New York. He received his advanced musical training at The American Conservatory of Music in Chicago and at the Mannes College of Music in New York. The diversity of his composing ranges from solos to orchestra works, in both vocal and instrumental music. Since 1982 he has received 25 grants from the Meet-the-Composer Foundation. His numerous compositions and arrangements have been published by various prominent educational and performance music publishers.

THE SLEEP OF THE CHILD JESUS

PIANO/CONDUCTOR/OBOE

FRANÇOIS GEVAERT, France

THE ANGELS AND THE SHEPHERDS

Bohemia

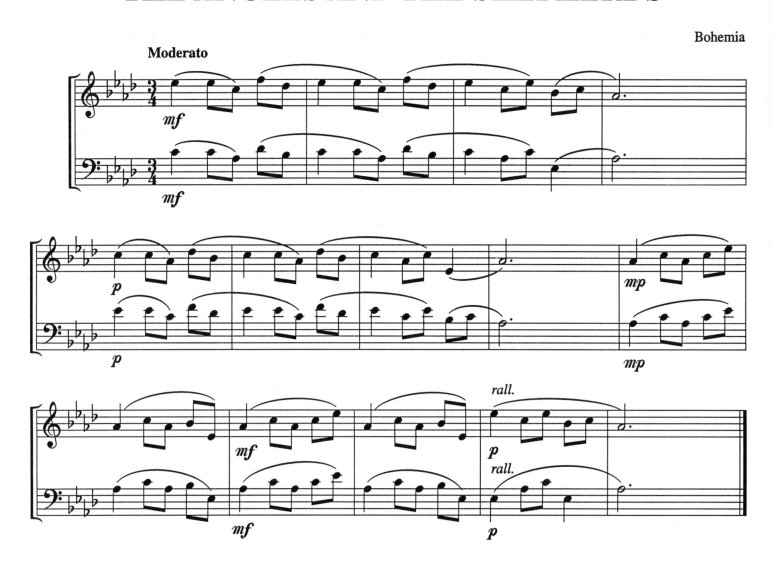

UNTO US IS BORN A SON

Tune from PIAE CANTIONES, 1582, England

A CHILD THIS DAY IS BORN

England

O COME, O COME, EMMANUEL

Plainsong Chant

IT CAME UPON THE MIDNIGHT CLEAR

RICHARD S. WILLIS, America

EL9554

SILENT NIGHT

FRANZ GRUBER, Germany

Gently

O CHRISTMAS TREE
(O Tannenbaum)

Germany

O SANCTISSIMA

Sicily

I SAW THREE SHIPS

England

O COME, ALL YE FAITHFUL

From J. F. WADE'S CANTUS DIVERSI

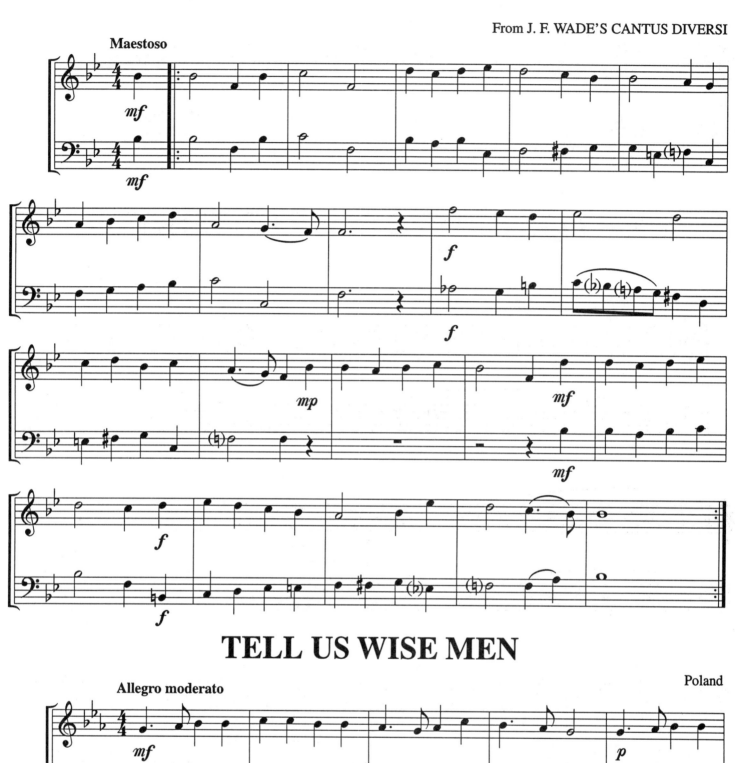

TELL US WISE MEN

Poland

O LITTLE TOWN OF BETHLEHEM

LEWIS H. REDNER, America

THE BABE IN BETHLEM'S MANGER LAID

England

DECK THE HALL

Old Welsh

THE NEW-BORN BABE

Spiritual

GOOD KING WENCESLAS

JOHN MASON NEALE, England

16

WHAT YOU GONNA CALL YOUR PRETTY LITTLE BABY?

Spiritual

FUM, FUM, FUM!

Catalonia

HARK! WHAT MEAN THOSE HOLY VOICES?

Russian melody

MASTERS IN THIS HALL

WILLIAM MORRIS, England

Allegro maestoso

BORN TODAY IS THE CHILD DIVINE
(Il Est Né)

France

Allegretto con moto

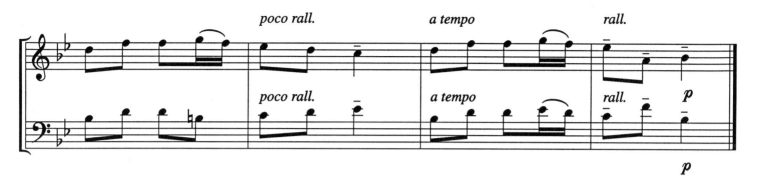

ROCKING

Czechoslovakia

MARCH OF THE THREE KINGS

GEORGES BIZET, France

A LA MEDIA NOCHE
(At the Hour of Midnight)

Puerto Rico

PATAPAN

France